GREEN FILES

POLLUTED PLANET

GREEN FILES – POLLUTED PLANET
was produced by

David West 👫 **Children's Books**
7 Princeton Court
55 Felsham Road
London SW15 1AZ

Editor: Gail Bushnell
Picture Research: Carlotta Cooper

First published in Great Britain by Heinemann
Library, Halley Court, Jordan Hill, Oxford
OX2 8EJ, part of Harcourt Education.
Heinemann is a registered trademark
of Harcourt Education Ltd.

07 06 05 04 03
10 9 8 7 6 5 4 3 2 1

ISBN 0 431 18291 4 (HB)
ISBN 0 431 18298 1 (PB)

British Library Cataloguing in Publication Data

Parker, Steve
Polluted planet. - (Green Files)
1. Pollution - Juvenile literature
2. Pollution prevention - Juvenile literature
I. Title
363.7'3

Printed and bound in Italy

*An explanation of difficult words can be
found in the glossary on page 31.*

GREEN FILES

POLLUTED PLANET

Steve Parker

Heinemann
LIBRARY

CONTENTS

Restless oceans spread pollution around the globe, carrying rubbish and chemicals thousands of kilometres to remote seashores.

Today's industries give us endless products, machines, gadgets and comforts, but at the cost of turning landscapes into polluted wastelands.

INTRODUCTION

Almost everywhere we look, there is pollution. Yet often, we don't see it. Some forms of pollution are invisible, such as rain water that contains acids, or toxic chemicals seeping into soil. Other types of pollution are so familiar that we hardly notice, like fumes from cars, or a local river empty of life. Few places on Earth are pollution-free. But with time and effort, the world can be made cleaner and safer from this modern menace.

Nuclear power stations make huge amounts of wastes polluted with radioactivity, and no one knows how to dispose of them.

Pollution is anything that causes harm, trouble or problems in our surroundings, or environment. It is also part of modern living. As we eat, learn, work, travel and enjoy ourselves, we either make pollution or contribute to it.

POLLUTION BY SUBSTANCES

Some pollution is in the form of substances and chemicals. These might be liquids, gases, or objects made from metals, plastics and similar materials. Pollution occurs when these substances collect where they should not be.

Electricity is our most convenient form of energy. But making and distributing it cause immense amounts of pollution.

THE WORLD GLOWS BRIGHTER

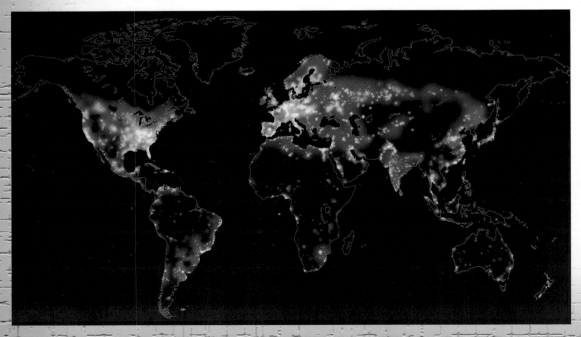

Endless lights from street lamps, buildings, advertising, vehicles and sports stadiums, flood the night sky with a bright glow – especially in built-up regions of the world. This form of energy pollution causes many difficulties. Some people cannot sleep in the 'twilight'. Bats and owls find it too bright for their delicate eyes. Astronomers cannot see the stars.

Hot topic

In the early 2000s a giant new pollution problem appeared in the skies over South and South East Asia. Called the Asian brown haze, it is a mix of smoke caused by fires and fumes from vehicles, factories and power stations.

The brown haze stays for days.

Every few years an oil tanker accident causes a polluting oil slick. But even more oil drips into the sea from broken pipes and leaky taps.

ENERGY POLLUTION

Pollution is also caused by forms of energy, such as heat, light, sound and radiation or radioactivity. These cause problems in the environment – and not only for people. For example, noisy boats on waterways mean that rare river dolphins cannot find food using their 'sonar' or sound echoes.

Noise pollution comes from vehicles, trains, planes and machines. It makes people feel tense, stressed, worried and ill.

Shops and stores are filled with an endless range of goods and products. But such choice and convenience has a terrible price – a plundered, polluted planet.

STARTING MATERIALS

Industry and manufacturing need raw materials, such as rocks called ores which contain metals, and minerals like sulphur. Mining or quarrying these causes much pollution.

Quarries and mines (left) leave ugly scars on the land. Rain water washes away the exposed rock minerals, which were deep in the ground, and these pollute rivers.

The use of natural resources, and the pollution caused by obtaining them, is greatly reduced by recycling – especially glass, but also metals, plastics and paper.

MASS PRODUCTION

Earth's raw materials and resources are changed greatly by manufacturing. They are processed into all kinds of plastics, metals, chemicals and other materials, which do not exist in nature. These are used by industry and end up as a vast array of items coming off mass production lines. Usually, the items are used for a time – then thrown away. The plastics, chemicals and other unnatural substances in them collect and cause environmental problems. Industry also uses huge amounts of energy from sources such as coal and oil, and these too cause many forms of pollution.

Superstores provide vast choices of foods and produce. But modern 'intensive' farming brings greater pollution to the countryside.

As technology and manufacturing advance, factories become out of date and useless – dangerous, decaying hulks of pollution.

Being GREEN

Some natural resources are renewable and cause little pollution. After a forest is cut for timber, it is planted with young trees for the future. Wood is a natural material and after use it rots back into the soil, avoiding problems of waste disposal.

Sustainable use of wood, where trees are replaced.

One of the most visible and harmful forms of pollution is dirty air. We cannot see through the dust, smog and particles it contains, and we breathe its poisonous chemicals into our delicate airways and lungs.

PARTICULATE POLLUTION

Some pollutants in air are too small to see. Larger particles (bits) float and blow around like smoky dust. They blot out the view, clog up air filters and delicate machines, and also get into our bodies to cause serious illness. Older diesel engines produce much particulate pollution.

Photochemical smog forms when polluting chemicals, especially from vehicle exhausts, change in sunlight. They clump into bigger particles.

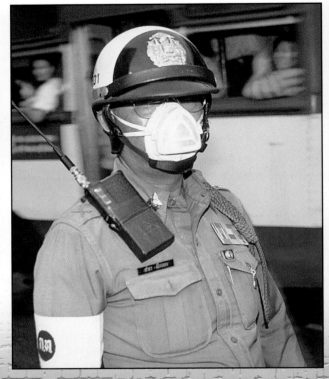

Statues from ancient times are now being eaten away in just a few years by the damaging, corrosive chemicals in city air (above). In Japan, traffic policemen wear masks to protect their lungs (right).

In some cities, air pollution is so bad that clothes have built-in air filters for safer breathing.

Hot topic

Air pollution is usually worst in built-up areas during warm, sunny, calm weather. City-dwellers suffer a great range of illnesses such as colds, coughs, wheezing and asthma, and lung infections like bronchitis and pneumonia.

Hills around Mexico City trap its polluted air.

FAR AND WIDE

Air pollution is a special problem because it does not stay in one place. Winds and weather carry it huge distances, so that people far away suffer its harmful effects.

CATS TO THE RESCUE

CATS, catalytic converters, are fitted to exhaust pipes of most new vehicles. They prevent some pollutants escaping into the air. They use special metals such as palladium to speed up, or catalyze, certain chemical reactions. Hydrocarbons (HCs) and deadly carbon monoxide (CO) are changed using oxygen (O_2) in the air, to water (H_2O) and less harmful carbon dioxide (CO_2).

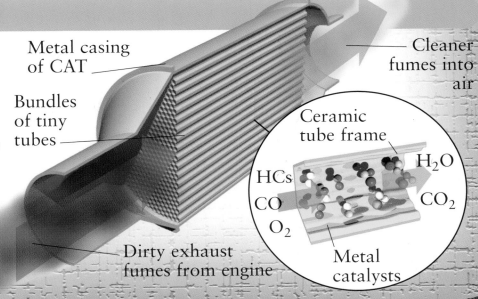

Metal casing of CAT

Bundles of tiny tubes

Cleaner fumes into air

Ceramic tube frame

HCs
CO
O_2

H_2O

CO_2

Metal catalysts

Dirty exhaust fumes from engine

Two kinds of air pollution, in particular, cause global problems. They are known as acid rain and ozone depletion. Some steps have been taken to limit the damage, but there is still much to do.

RAINING ACIDS

Smoke and fumes often contain a mixture of chemicals, including oxides of sulphur and nitrogen. They float into the air and dissolve in the tiny droplets of water which make up clouds, forming chemicals which are acidic and harmful. The cloud droplets eventually merge and fall as raindrops. The acids in the rain soak into soil and streams, and damage trees and water life such as fish.

Devices such as filters and scrubbers are now fitted to many chimneys and smoke-stacks, to capture or trap some of the acid-forming chemicals.

BATHED IN ACID

The main causes of acid rain are the smoke and fumes from power stations, factory chimneys and vehicle exhausts. In the moisture and droplets of clouds they form a mix of different acids.

Acid-forming chemicals in fumes

Trees suffer greatly from acid rain. The chemicals in the drops 'burn' their leaves and make their roots unable to take up nutrients.

The polluted clouds can blow great distances on the wind before they release their moisture as acid rain. So the damage may happen far away from the original polluters, in remote wilderness areas.

Wind   Acid rain

CFCs *in fridge cooling fluids need careful disposal.*

CULPRIT CFCs

Ozone is a form of oxygen spread thinly in air. It helps to protect the Earth from the Sun's more harmful rays, especially UV (ultra-violet) radiation. CFC (chlorofluorocarbon) chemicals get into the air from some kinds of aerosols and industrial processes. They destroy ozone, reducing its protective effect. This puts living things at risk from diseases such as cancer.

2001   *2002*

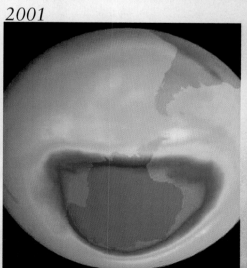
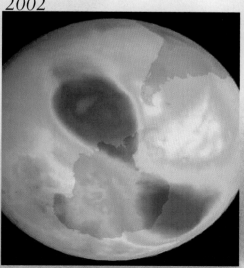

Being GREEN

Most aerosol sprays are now CFC-free, as shown by their labels. But they still contain many different chemicals, and making the pressure-cans uses up natural resources. Pump-type sprays usually cause less harm to the environment.

Help the world: be CFC-free.

The way the world's winds and climate work, mean that ozone loss is greatest over the South Pole. Computer images show how the ozone 'hole', where damage is worst (red-blue), varies from year to year.

13

Plants that grow in soil (earth or 'dirt') are the main foods of people around the world. Animals such as cattle and sheep eat plants too, and people eat their meat. So polluted soils affect our foods, and us – and, of course, wildlife.

THE '-ICIDES'

Insecticides, herbicides and fungicides are chemicals sprayed on to farm plants or watered into their soil. The aim is to make the plants grow faster and better. However …

Some soil is so polluted that it is removed as a hazard to human life (below). But where is it dumped?

Soil is so important to growing food, and to the natural world. Scientists collect samples (right) and analyze them for polluting chemicals (below).

LASTING PROBLEMS

... Some of these chemicals can last for years. They kill small creatures such as caterpillars, worms and mites, who normally help to keep the soil healthy. Certain chemicals are taken up by plants into their stems, leaves and flowers. Animals eat the plants and the chemicals collect in their bodies too. At any stage the pollution can cause harm. Sometimes this is not obvious for many years, until the damage is widespread.

In India, tea bushes (above) are sprayed to kill pests. But the workers lack protection and may be at risk.

Protesters warn of GM dangers.

Hot topic

Genetic Modification, or GM, aims to improve the genes of farm plants and animals. But these new genes could escape into weeds and soil animals, causing unexpected changes.

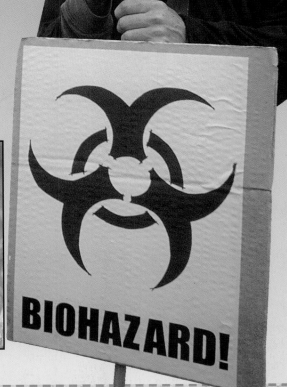

GM crops are tested in fields.

15

Water is vital for life and a most precious resource. It is an excellent solvent – substances dissolve or spread through it – and it is always on the move. It falls as rain, flows in streams and rivers to the sea, and soaks into soil. However, it can create problems.

THE PROBLEM IS THE SOLUTION

Water dissolves all kinds of chemicals and pollutants, and then spreads them far and wide. As the pollutants are carried about, they may affect aquatic life such as fish and waterbirds, who die from their toxic effects.

Some water pollution is obvious, like acid in a French stream and debris at an Estonian power station. But much is unseen and invisible.

SOURCES OF WATER POLLUTION

Some rivers are like continually flowing dustbins that carry away wastes, chemicals and other pollutants. But these substances do not disappear. They harm river life downstream. They collect in lakes and reach even more dangerous levels. Or the water is taken for irrigation, spreading the pollution to our fields and farms.

Farming
Pesticides, herbicides and other chemicals are washed by rain into rivers.

Industry
Wastes and effluents pour from discharge pipes.

People
Water flows down drains and toilets, into the treatment and disposal system.

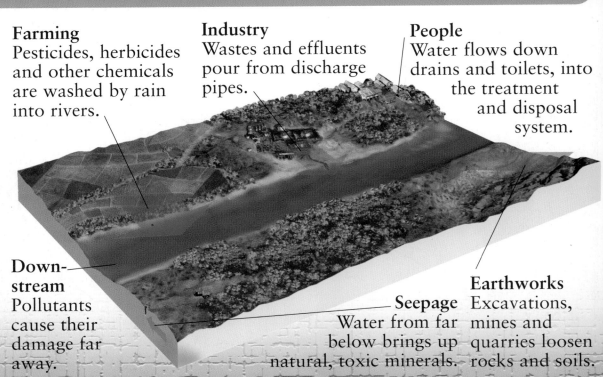

Down-stream
Pollutants cause their damage far away.

Seepage
Water from far below brings up natural, toxic minerals.

Earthworks
Excavations, mines and quarries loosen rocks and soils.

Hot topic

The Ganges of India is one of world's largest, most sacred and most heavily used rivers. Millions of people wash, bathe, take water supplies and dispose of waste here. The river is the subject of massive anti-pollution and clean-up campaigns.

Bathing in the Ganges: a religious ritual.

ACCIDENTALLY ON PURPOSE

Some chemicals get into water by accident, from broken pipes or mistakenly opened taps at factories. But huge amounts of pollutants are also dumped on purpose into rivers, lakes and seas, in the hope that they will spread out and become lost. Some of them, however, will last hundreds of years.

Too much of a good thing – fertilizers washed into rivers and the sea become food for tiny life-forms that cause a poisonous 'red tide'.

Many cases of oil pollution are deliberate. Some ships wash out their tanks, hoping no one notices.

17

Radioactivity (radiation) is a form of energy given off by certain chemical substances, from their tiniest parts – atoms. It is invisible, but it can be deadly. Some types of radioactivity will last for thousands of years.

SOURCES OF RADIOACTIVITY

The main sources of radioactivity are the nuclear industry, especially nuclear or atomic power stations, and the weapons industry that makes nuclear missiles and atomic bombs. Small amounts are also used in medicine and scientific research.

TYPES OF RADIATION

Various natural substances emit radioactivity, but in very small amounts. It becomes much stronger when radioactive elements such as uranium and plutonium are purified and processed for nuclear power stations and weapons. They give off three forms of energy. Alpha and beta particles are bits of atoms, while gamma radiation is wave-like rays.

Whole atom

Electron

Nucleus

Alpha particle (one proton and one neutron)

Gamma rays

Beta particle (one electron)

Regular safety checks monitor any low levels of radiation leaking from nuclear sites.

DANGERS OF RADIATION

Radiation can cause sickness, skin sores, burns, tumours, cancers and many other forms of illness – not only to people, but to animals, and damage to plant life. Most nuclear sites take great care that radiation does not escape. But there have been several accidents over the years. In 1986 at Chernobyl in Ukraine, a power station exploded and polluted vast areas with radioactive dust. Hundreds of people died as a result. Lower levels of radioactivity can also leak into air and water, and build up in the soil.

Sites such as England's Sellafield handle many radioactive substances, as they process nuclear fuels and use them to generate electricity. If an accident occurs and radiation escapes, there is no way of gathering the pollution back again.

Nuclear waste accumulates daily around the world. There is no safe, long-term way of disposing of it, so for now, it is simply stored.

Being GREEN

World leaders hold meetings to reduce numbers of nuclear weapons. But the radioactive material in them can only be stored, not destroyed. Governments must prevent terrorists obtaining this radioactive material for making weapons such as 'dirty bombs'.

Presidents Putin (Russia) and Bush (USA).

People often say: 'Something should be done about pollution'. We may say it ourselves. But really pollution is everyone's problem, and we can all do something about it. We can start in our daily lives, in homes, schools, offices and factories.

HOUSEHOLD CHEMICALS

Everything we tip down the sink or toilet goes into the water-treatment and sewage systems. Powerful chemicals such as bleaches and strong cleansers force these systems to work harder.

HOW HOMES HELP

The modern kitchen's labour-saving gadgets are convenient – but often waste energy and resources. It also costs money and energy to bring clean water in, and to take it away for treatment after use.

Friendly help
Some detergents, soaps and cleaners are friendlier to the environment.

ECOLOGICAL
LAUNDRY BLEACH
ECOVER
KEEPS WHITES BRIGHT
NATURALLY
CHLORINE FREE

The contents of the trashcan and dustbin must go somewhere – often into landfill sites, which may only store pollution for the future.

Too-hot spot
Turn heaters off and save energy.

Recyclable material
Keep suitable containers in handy places to make recycling easier.

Most stores stock environment-friendly products. They are made using fewer natural resources, more recycled materials and less energy. So they also reduce pollution and clear-up 'after-costs'.

Hot topic

Public transport can be quick, safe and less harmful to our environment. Yet many transport systems are crowded, dirty and expensive. More people can be encouraged to use public transport if it is reliable, efficient, and comfortable.

A weather-proof bus shelter in Brazil.

Electric economy
Switch off electrical devices when they are not needed and reduce pollution at the power station.

Drain strain
Turn taps off and avoid wasting water twice over – supply and disposal.

Solar cells trap 'free' light energy to charge batteries in electric vehicles, preventing much pollution.

More trams mean less jams, accidents and noise as well as less pollution.

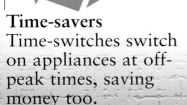

Time-savers
Time-switches switch on appliances at off-peak times, saving money too.

OUT AND ABOUT

A person travelling by public transport such as bus, tram or train, causes up to 100 times less pollution than a person driving alone in a car. Many cities are developing electric trains, trams and monorails, which do not pump harmful exhaust gases into the air and also reduce noise pollution.

CAN INDUSTRY HELP?

Factories and industries make products that people buy, and also make profits so that they stay in business and provide jobs. But it is often difficult to be successful in industry, yet also avoid pollution.

Iron, steel and electronics industries are huge users of resources, so recycling is especially important.

THE MAIN AIM

Industry and mass production help us by making consumer goods for our convenience. They can also help us by finding new ways of reducing harm to the environment. Many countries now have anti-pollution regulations, but sometimes industries find sneaky ways around these.

Every few years leaders gather for an 'Earth Summit' to discuss issues such as poverty and pollution. But in 2002 in Johannesburg, South Africa, little progress was made.

Being GREEN

In the 1970s-80s concerns grew about the substance lead in vehicle fuels such as petrol. Lead made engines run more smoothly, but it also got into exhaust fumes and, if breathed in, possibly damaged the body's brain and nerve system. Most countries now have 'green' lead-free petrol – but this still releases dangerous substances into the air.

Lead-free petrol: better than leaded, but still polluting.

'POLLUTER PAYS'

As people become more aware of pollution dangers, laws and guidelines are changing. Formerly, it was necessary to prove that a polluting substance released by industry actually caused harm. More and more, it is now necessary for industry to prove that the substance does not cause harm, and also to pay for clean-ups or problems that result.

Filters and scrubbers on chimneys and power stations remove the most harmful chemicals and fumes. But this adds to the cost of production.

PEOPLE POLLUTION

The world has more than 6,000 million (six billion) people, and this number is rising faster every year. Most people want food, water, a place to live, and goods such as cars and televisions. So the demand for these products and resources is also rocketing. Is there a limit to what our world can provide?

POPULATION PRESSURE

Numbers of people are rising fastest in Asia, South America and Africa – places where millions already struggle against poverty, disease, hunger and polluted water supplies. Also numbers are rising much faster in cities than the countryside, and so overcrowding forces more pollution into less area.

Millions of People

Sao Paulo, Brazil
Buenos Aires, Brazil
Mexico City, Mexico
New York, USA
Istanbul, Turkey
Mumbai, India
Karachi, Pakistan
Moscow, Russian Fed.
Delhi, India
Dhaka, Bangladesh
Jakarta, Indonesia
Manila, Philippines
Shanghai, China
Seoul, South Korea
Tokyo, Japan

North America
483 million

Europe
732 million

Asia
3,674 million

South America
342 million

Africa
778 million

Australia and Oceania
31 million

Some countries advise their citizens to have fewer children.

About 1/20th of the world's people own 19/20ths of the world's wealth. This imbalance forces millions to survive in shanties, slums and favelas, as seen here in Rio de Janeiro, Brazil.

CROWDED CITIES

Pollution problems are usually worse in cities where many people live close together and crowd into offices and factories. Even disposing of their bodily wastes is a huge challenge, so that sewage does not foul the air, pollute water and spread germs and disease.

Modern sewage works, such as this one in London, treat daily wastes and effluents from thousands of people, while causing minimal pollution.

Being GREEN

Many cities encourage people to cycle rather than use cars, by providing cycle lanes that are safe and follow direct, useful routes. This saves money, reduces pollution and is healthy exercise.

Cyclists in Paris, France.

RICH AND POOR

The populations in many rich countries are rising slowly, if at all, and there is money for a comfortable lifestyle and also to combat pollution. People in poorer areas see the lifestyle of the wealthy, and naturally they want it too. But they have less money to spend, especially on caring for the environment, and so pollution spirals out of control.

Winds and water currents carry pollution around the globe, even to remote mountain-tops and polar regions. Some of the pollutants greatly harm wildlife.

UNSEEN DANGER

Many types of chemical pollutants have found their way to wilderness areas, where they damage plants and animals. A particular hazard known as bio-accumulation is shown below.

Birds try to clean oil from their feathers using their beaks, but they swallow oil in the process, and soon die.

POLLUTANTS IN THE FOOD CHAIN

Levels of a pollutant may be so low in water that it is hardly noticed. But the chemical is taken in by plants, which are eaten by animals, who are in turn eaten, and so on along the food chain. At each stage the pollutant's level rises as it collects or accumulates in the body, then passes on. The animals at the end of the food chain accumulate high enough levels of pollutant to suffer harm.

1 Polluting chemicals are very spread out or dilute in sea water.

2 Plankton (tiny plants and animals) take in small amounts.

3 Small fish eat plankton and absorb more of the pollutants.

4 Seals eat many fish, accumulating even more.

5 Pollutants are higher still in polar bears who eat fish and seals.

A few sick seals recovered.

PROBLEM CHEMICALS

Examples of polluting chemicals include PCBs (polychlorinated biphenyls) used in industry and organochlorides in some pesticides and herbicides. These are not quickly biodegraded – they do not break down easily in nature after use into less harmful substances.

Pollution's effects may take years to show. The now-banned pesticide DDT collected in birds like peregrines and affected their eggs, so they could not breed.

Field trials of pesticides and herbicides check how much of the chemical gets into soil and how long it lasts.

MANY EFFECTS

Some pollutant chemicals have direct effects, causing sores on an animal's body or eyes. Others get into the body and weaken the animal's resistance, so it can no longer fight off germs, diseases and infesting parasites.

Some of the most dangerous effects of pollution are on our own bodies and minds. Chemicals in air, water, foods and drinks may get into the body and cause damage – sometimes permanent.

TICKING TIME-BOMB

Some effects of pollution on health are clear, such as chemicals that cause sickness and diarrhoea. Other pollutants may cause only a few minor problems at first, like dizziness or weakness. In time, the pollutants accumulate to high levels and can lead to serious problems.

People who live near busy roadways may suffer more breathing problems than average. They are tested using a peak-flow meter.

In poor and crowded regions, the effects of pollution may be difficult to distinguish from other health hazards, such as lack of food and water contaminated with germs.

A new well aims to bring clean water to an area. But some wells are polluted by natural substances like arsenic, which seep up from far underground.

NATURE LENDS A HAND

There is much research into ways of absorbing polluting chemicals from the environment naturally, using living things – especially simple plants like algae, microbes such as bacteria, and fungi like mushrooms. Some of these are being genetically modified to take in large amounts of the pollutant from their surroundings, without suffering harm. Then these living things can be collected and disposed of in a safe way.

Lichens (combinations of algae and fungi) take in certain pollutants from the air, like 'living sponges'.

POLLUTION AND THE BODY

Almost every part of the body is at risk from some kind of pollution. Airways and lungs are vulnerable to airborne fumes and particles, and the digestive system to chemicals in foods and drinks. Damage to the brain and nerves tends to happen more slowly.

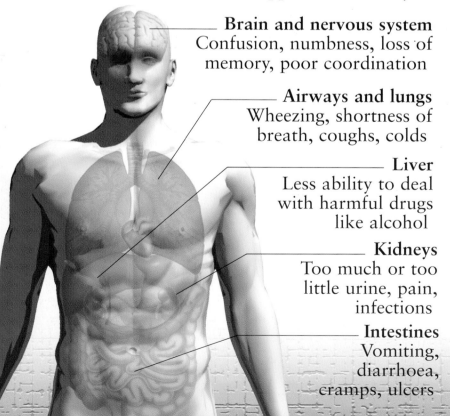

Brain and nervous system
Confusion, numbness, loss of memory, poor coordination

Airways and lungs
Wheezing, shortness of breath, coughs, colds

Liver
Less ability to deal with harmful drugs like alcohol

Kidneys
Too much or too little urine, pain, infections

Intestines
Vomiting, diarrhoea, cramps, ulcers

Hot topic

In the 1950s people near Minimata Bay, Japan, began to suffer mysterious problems such as trembling, poor muscle control and babies with birth defects. The cause was traced to the dangerous 'heavy metal' mercury. It was used by local industry, emptied into the bay and eaten by shellfish and fish, which the people then ate.

Minimata memorial, Japan

29

It's easy to blame pollution on everyone else. Yet we can all take action to reduce the problem and make our world safer and less polluted.

STEPS TO TAKE

In daily life around the home, at the shops, school and work, while travelling and spending our leisure time – we can be aware of pollution. There are many ways to tackle the problem: waste less, recycle more, conserve natural resources, choose environment-friendly products, support groups that identify polluters, and campaign for a cleaner, greener future in our world.

Addresses and websites for further information

AIR QUALITY (UK)
Freephone Air Pollution
Information Service
0800 556677
E-mail aqinfo@aeat.co.uk
www.airquality.co.uk
Information about air quality and pollution, including causes, local levels and possible action.

THE SOIL ASSOCIATION
Bristol House,
40-56 Victoria Street,
Bristol,
BS1 6BY
Tel 0117 929 0661
Fax 0117 925 2504
E-mail info@soilassociation.org
www.soilassociation.org
UK's leading campaigning and certification organization for organic food and farming
.

FRIENDS OF THE EARTH
26-28 Underwood Street,
London,
N1 7JQ
Tel 020 7490 1555
Fax 020 7490 0881
www.foe.co.uk
International network of environmental groups, who campaign for reduced levels of all kinds of pollution.

GREENPEACE UK
Canonbury Villas,
London,
N1 2PN
Tel 020 7865 8100
Fax 020 7865 8200
E-mail info@uk.greenpeace.org
www.greenpeace.org.uk
Campaigning organization who support action against polluters.

AUSTRALIAN GREENHOUSE OFFICE
GPO Box 621,
Canberra ACT 2601,
Australia
Tel 1800 130 606
Fax 02 9274 1390
www.greenhouse.gov.au

UK RIVERS NETWORK
www.ukrivers.net/pollution
Problems of water pollution, the causes and solutions.

ENVIRONMENT PROTECTION AUTHORITY
Environment Australia,
GPO Box 787,
Canberra ACT 2601
Australia
Tel 02 6274 1111
Fax 02 6274 1666
www.environment.gov.au

GLOSSARY

CAT
Catalytic convertor, a device that removes some harmful substances and pollutants from the exhaust gases of cars and other vehicles.

CFCs
Chlorofluorocarbons, industrial chemicals which have an especially damaging effect on ozone in the atmosphere.

environment
The surroundings including soil, rocks, water, air, plants, animals and even man-made structures.

ore
Rocks or similar substances from the Earth which contain useful amounts of minerals or metals, such as iron, aluminium or sulphur.

ozone
A form of the gas oxygen, which is spread through the atmosphere and helps to protect the Earth's surface against some of the Sun's damaging ultra-violet rays.

PCBs
Polychlorinated biphenyls, chemicals from industry that can harm living things.

pesticide
A substance designed to kill or disable pests such as insects or worms, especially on farm crops or animals.

pollutant
A substance that causes harm or damage to our surroundings, including wildlife and ourselves.

recycle
To use something again, or to take it apart or break it up, and use the substances it was made from again.

smog
A combination of fumes, particles and gases, especially from vehicle exhausts, that causes a harmful haze in the air.

toxic
Harmful, poisonous or damaging.